DATE DUE

ETT

Z0040800   12/95

A ROOKIE READER

EAT YOUR PEAS, LOUISE!

By Pegeen Snow

Illustrations by Mike Venezia

Prepared under the direction of Robert Hillerich, Ph.D.

 CHILDRENS PRESS ™

CHICAGO

To MARION RICHARDSON
aunt, friend, poet

Library of Congress Cataloging in Publication Data

Snow, Pegeen.
  Eat your peas, Louise.

  (A Rookie Reader)
  Summary: Louise is given all sorts of reasons for eating
her peas.
  1. Children's stories, American. [1. Peas—Fiction.
2. Food—Fiction. 3. Stories in rhyme]
I. Venezia, Mike, ill. II. Title. III. Series.
PZ8.3.3S673Eat   1985   [E]   84-27445
ISBN 0-516-02067-6

8 9 10 11 12 13 14 15 16 17 R 02 01 00 99 98 97 96 95 94

"Eat your peas, Louise.
You will like good peas like these."   3

"How fat and round they are!
Just squeeze!"

"Will you eat them if
I add some cheese?"

8

"Eat them with your fork, or. . ."

"Eat them with your spoon."

11

"But eat them up fast.
It's way past noon."

"Eat them and you may fish with me."

"Or climb a tree."

"Or watch TV."

19

"Eat them when I count to three."

"One. . . two. . ."

"Oh, me!"

"Don't be a tease, Louise!
Eat your peas!"

"Please?"

WORD LIST

a	fork	or	tree
add	good	past	two
and	how	peas	TV
are	I	please	up
be	if	round	watch
but	it's	some	way
cheese	just	spoon	when
climb	like	squeeze	will
count	Louise	tease	with
don't	may	them	you
eat	me	these	your
fast	noon	they	
fat	oh	three	
fish	one	to	

About the Author

Eat Your Peas, Louise is the third book by **Pegeen Snow** to be published by Childrens Press. Another Rookie Reader by Ms. Snow is *A Pet for Pat.* In addition, her short stories and light verse have appeared in a variety of publications. A native of Eau Claire, Wisconsin, Ms. Snow's non-writing interests include "noodling at the piano, de-fleaing the cats, and trying to fix up an obstinate house."

About the Artist

Eat Your Peas, Louise is the sixth book illustrated by **Mike Venezia** for Childrens Press. the others are *Sometimes I Worry, What If The Teacher Calls On Me?, Ask A Silly Question, Rugs Have Naps,* and *The I Don't Want To Go To School Book.* Mike is a graduate of the School of The Art Institute of Chicago. When not working on children's books, Mike is a busy Chicago art director and father of Michael Anthony and Elizabeth Ann.